I0488539

Copyright © 2015 Skelly O.

All Rights Reserved Worldwide

SKULLS
Coloring Book

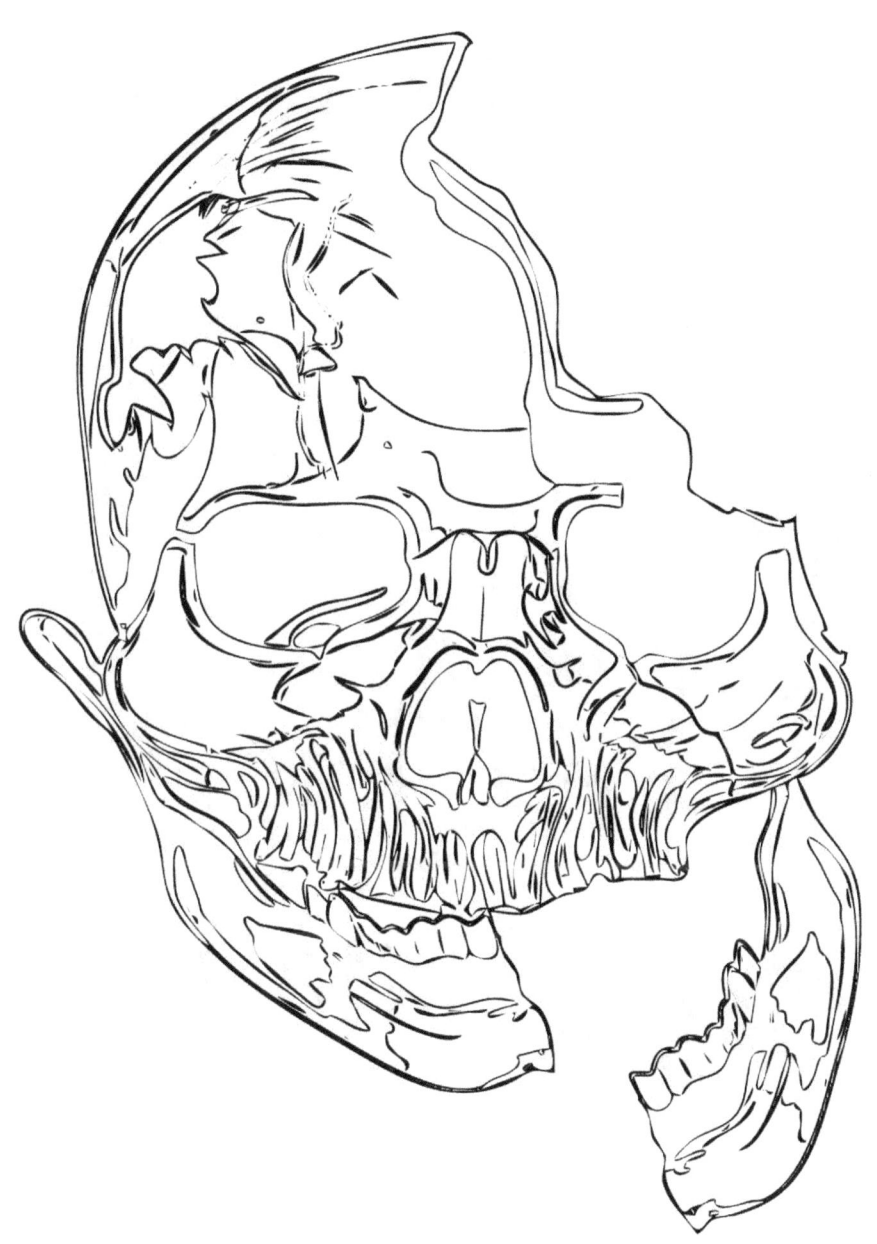

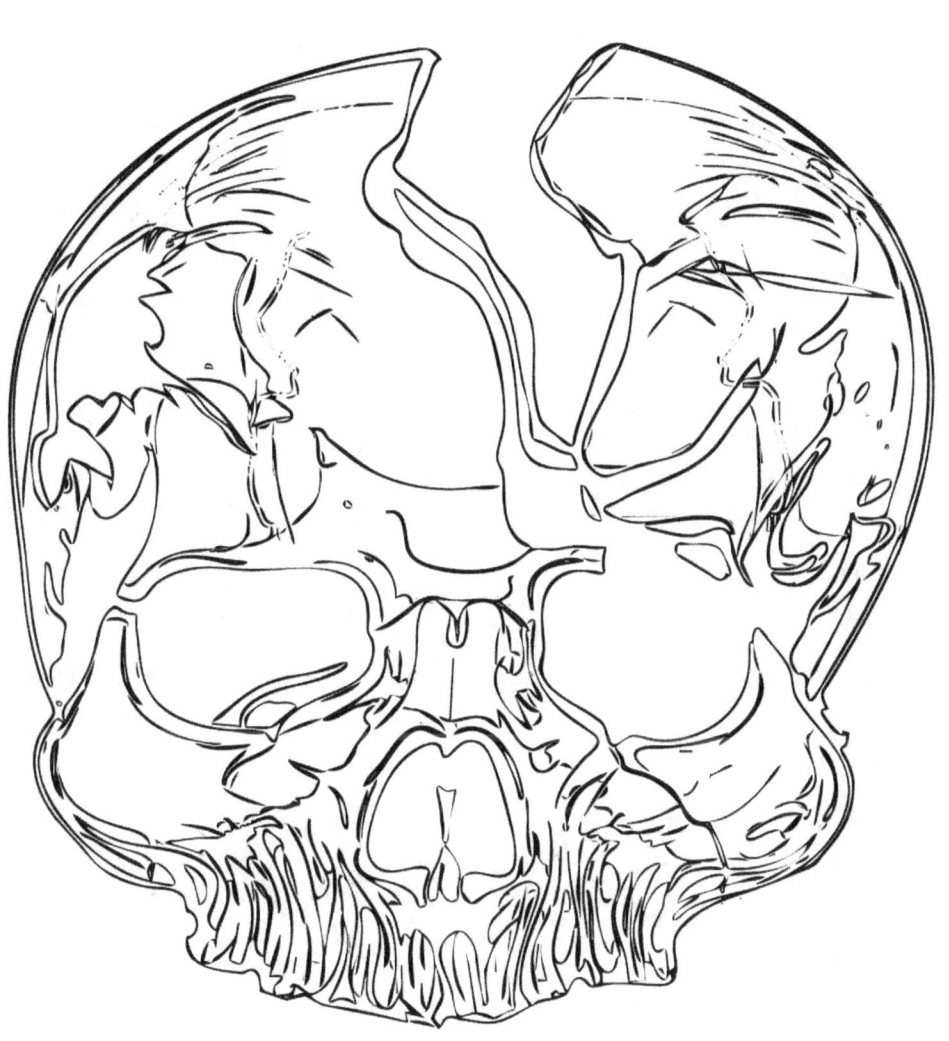

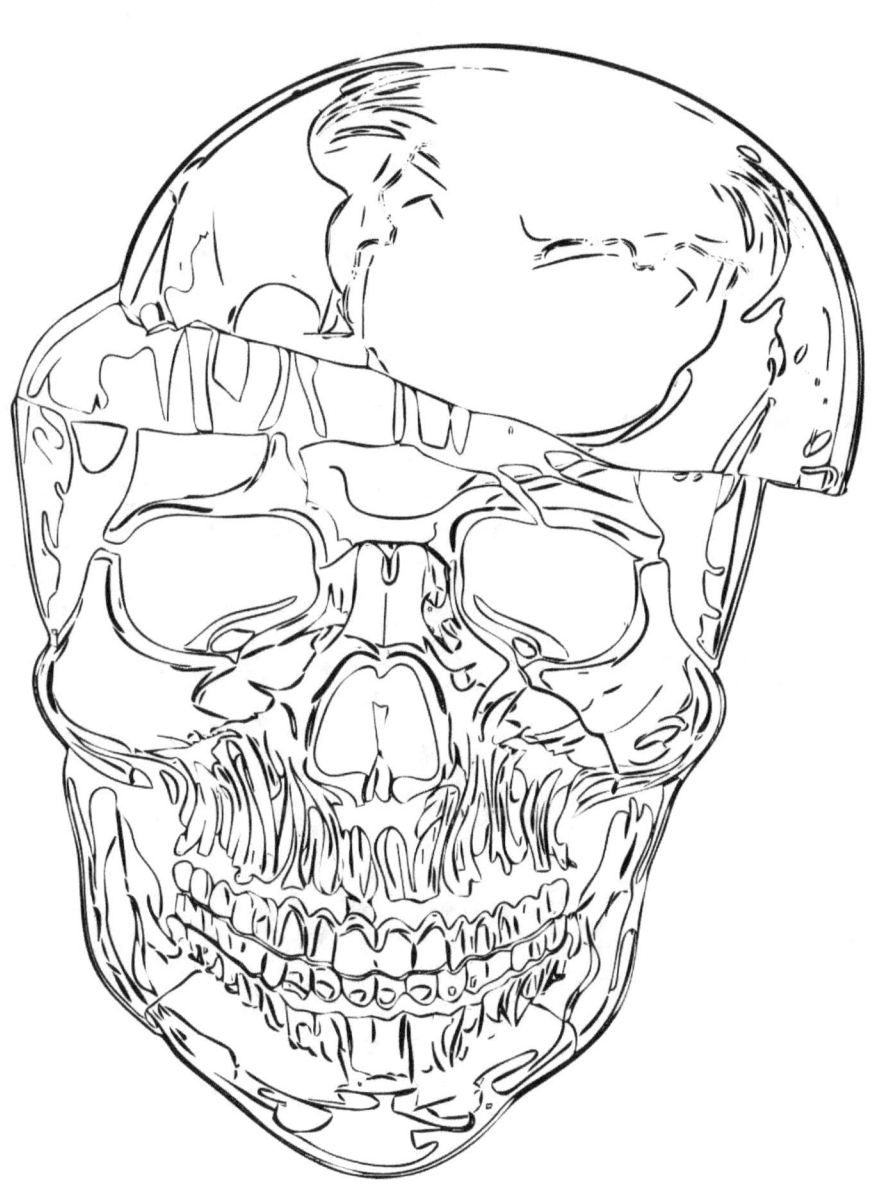

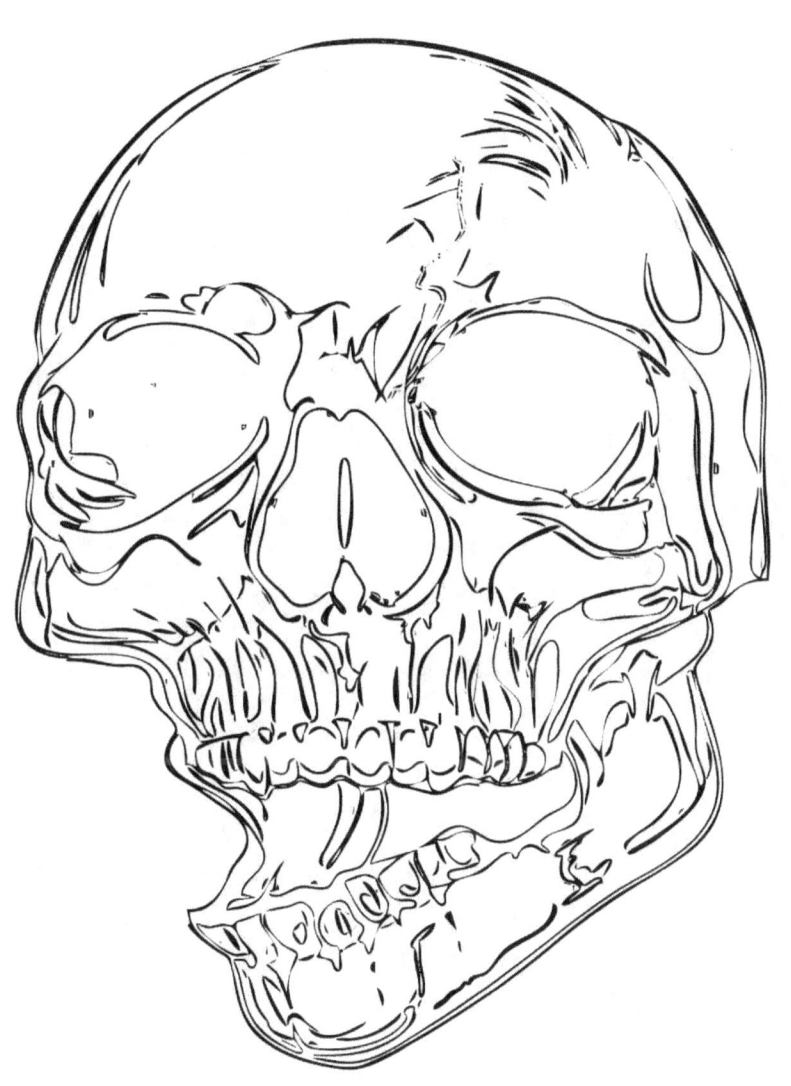

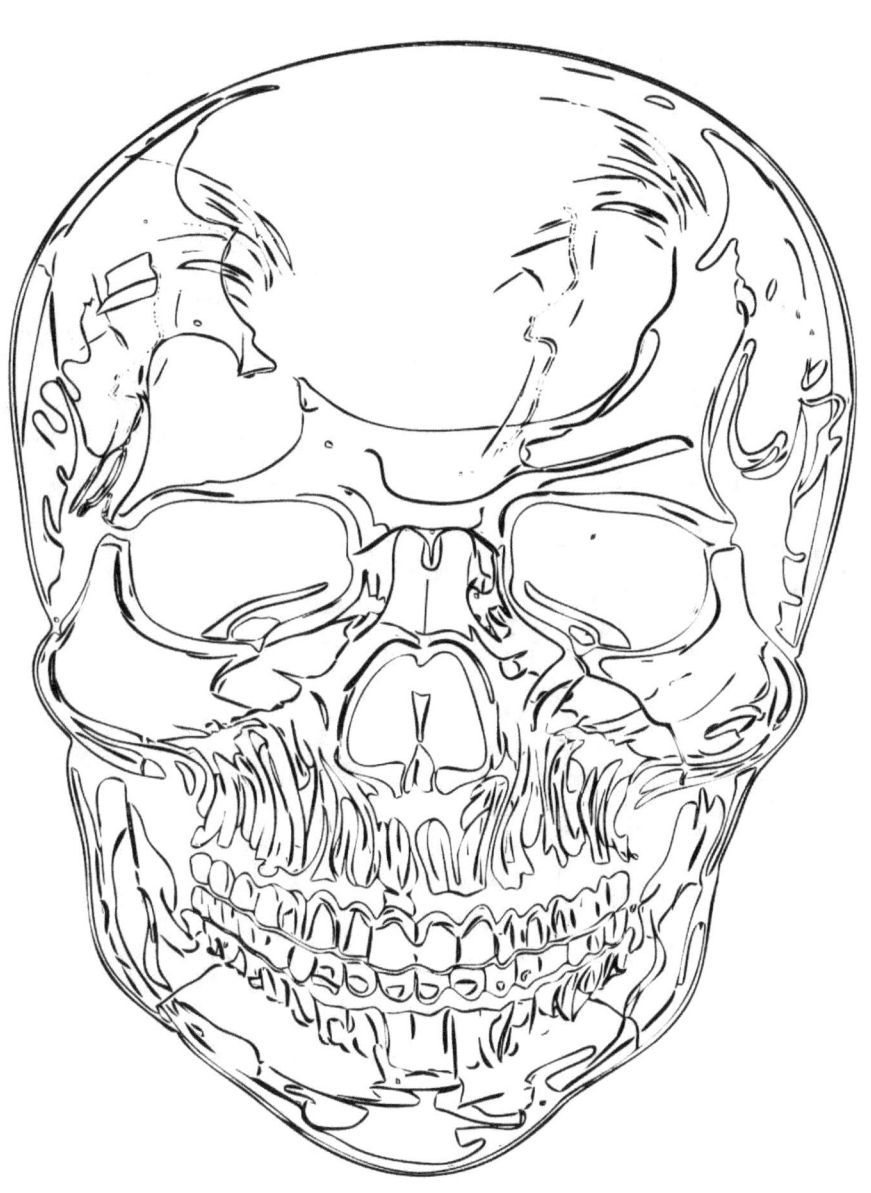

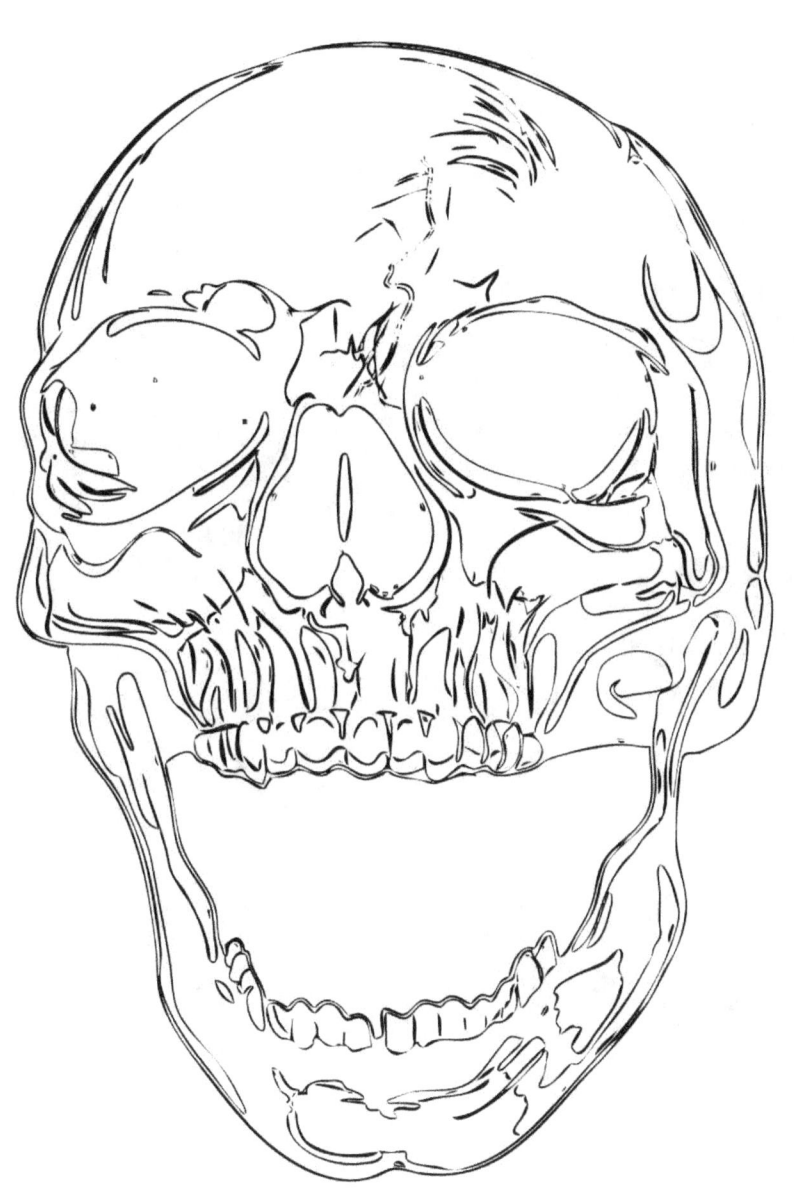

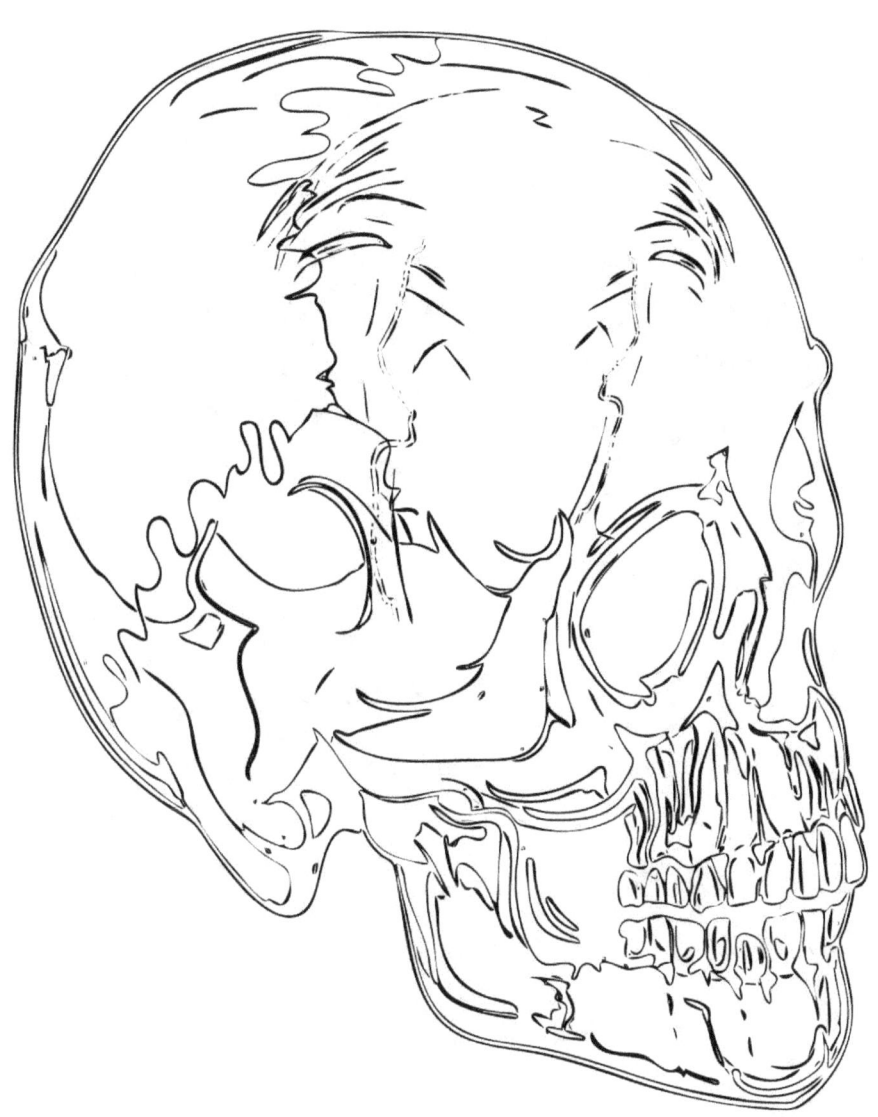

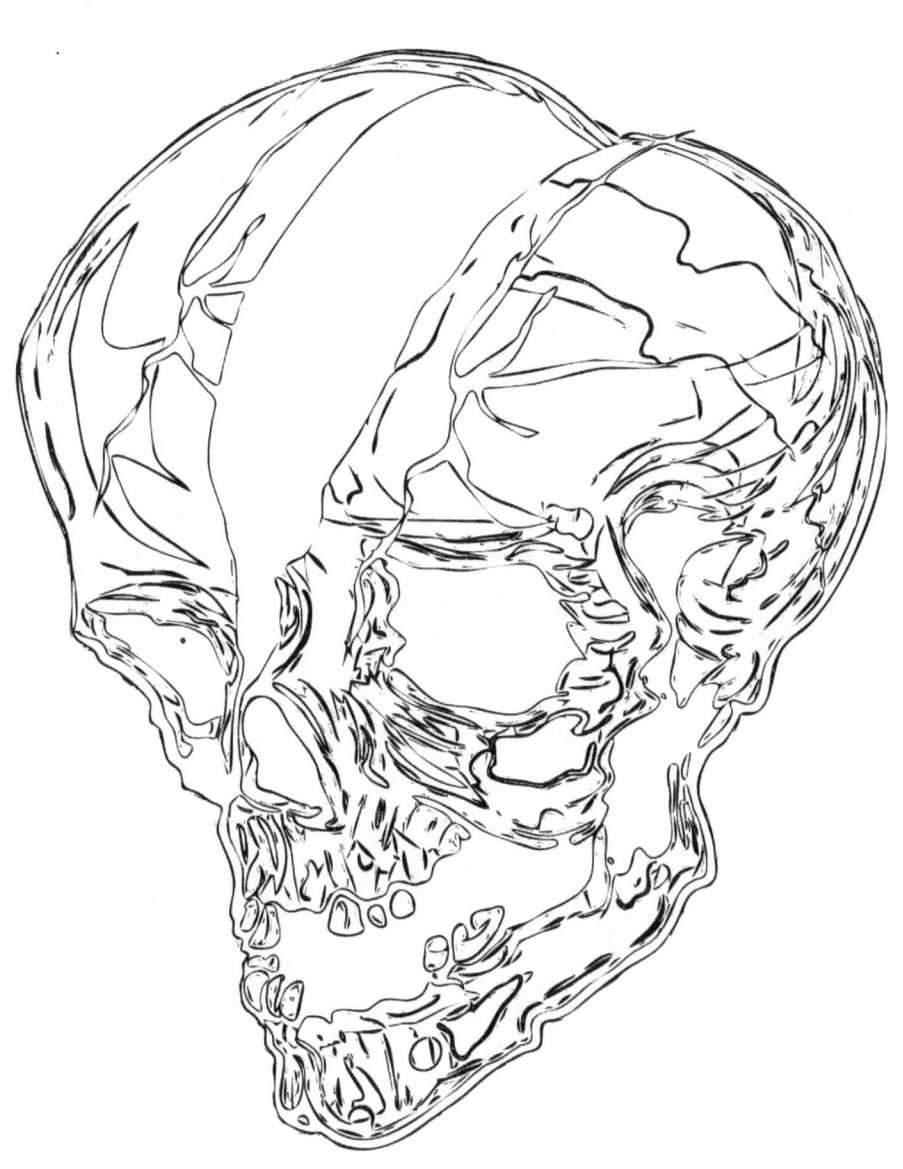

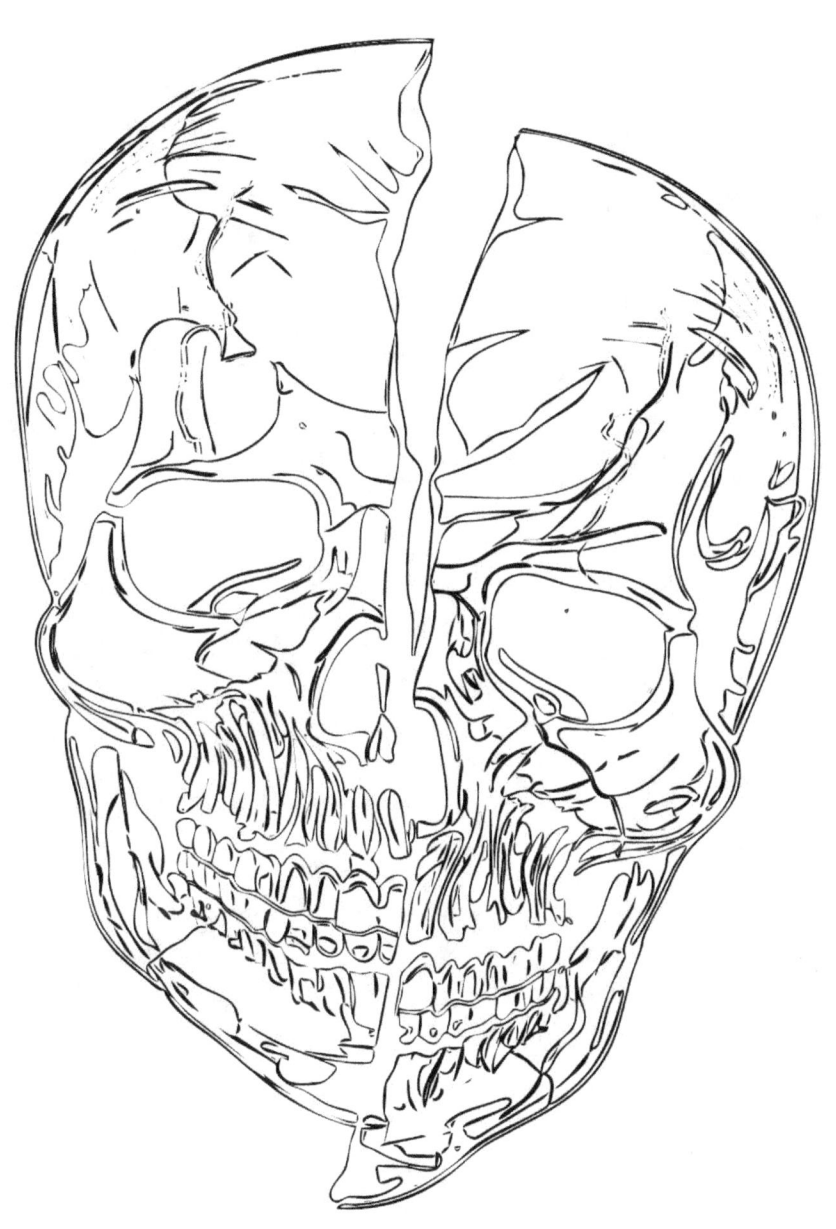

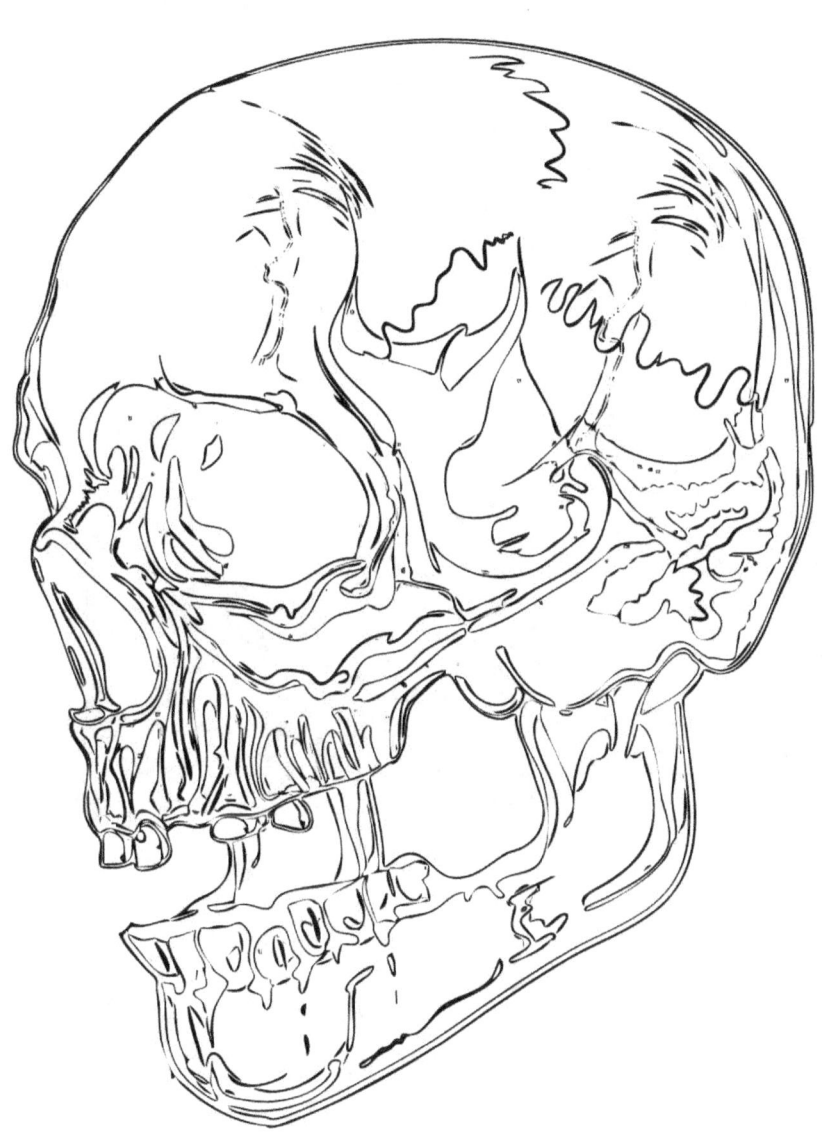

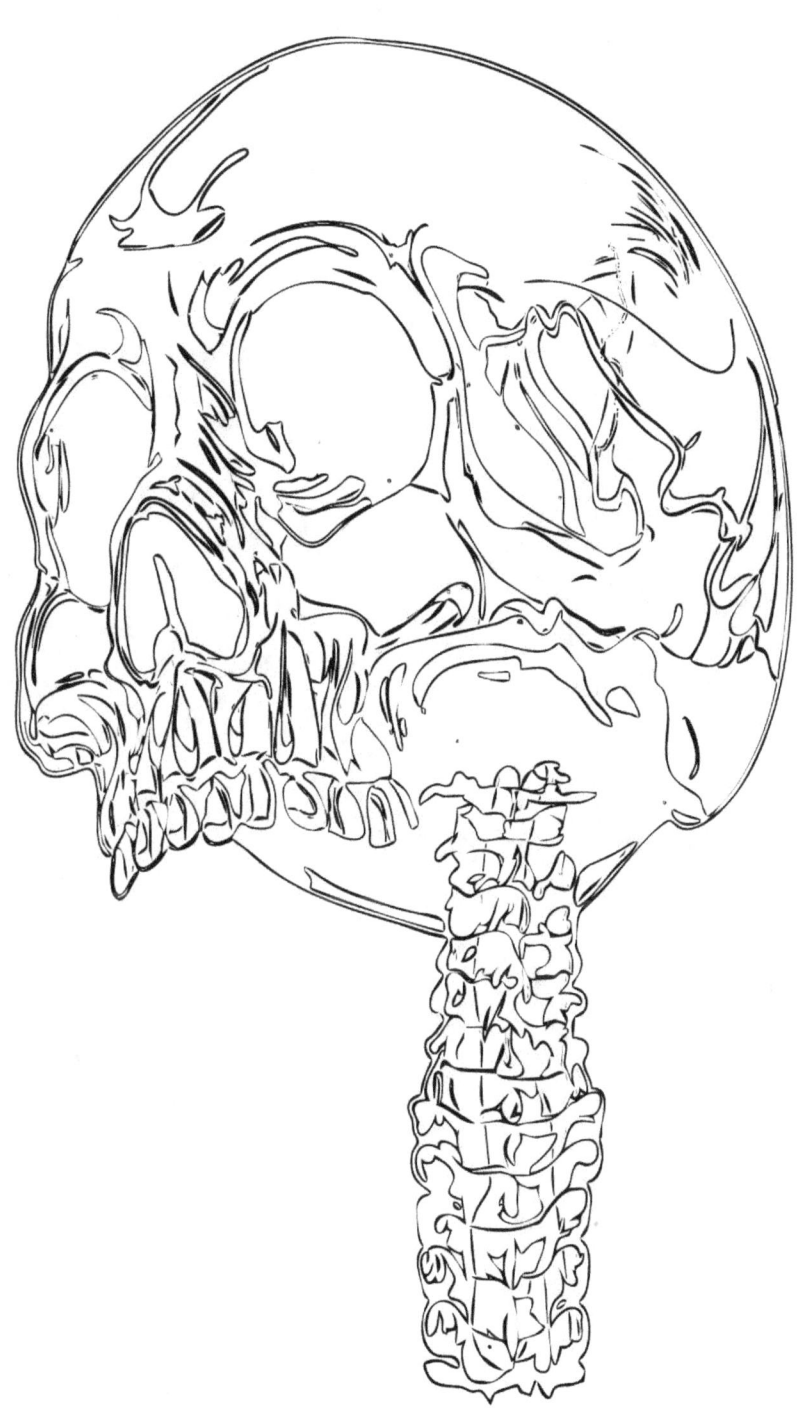

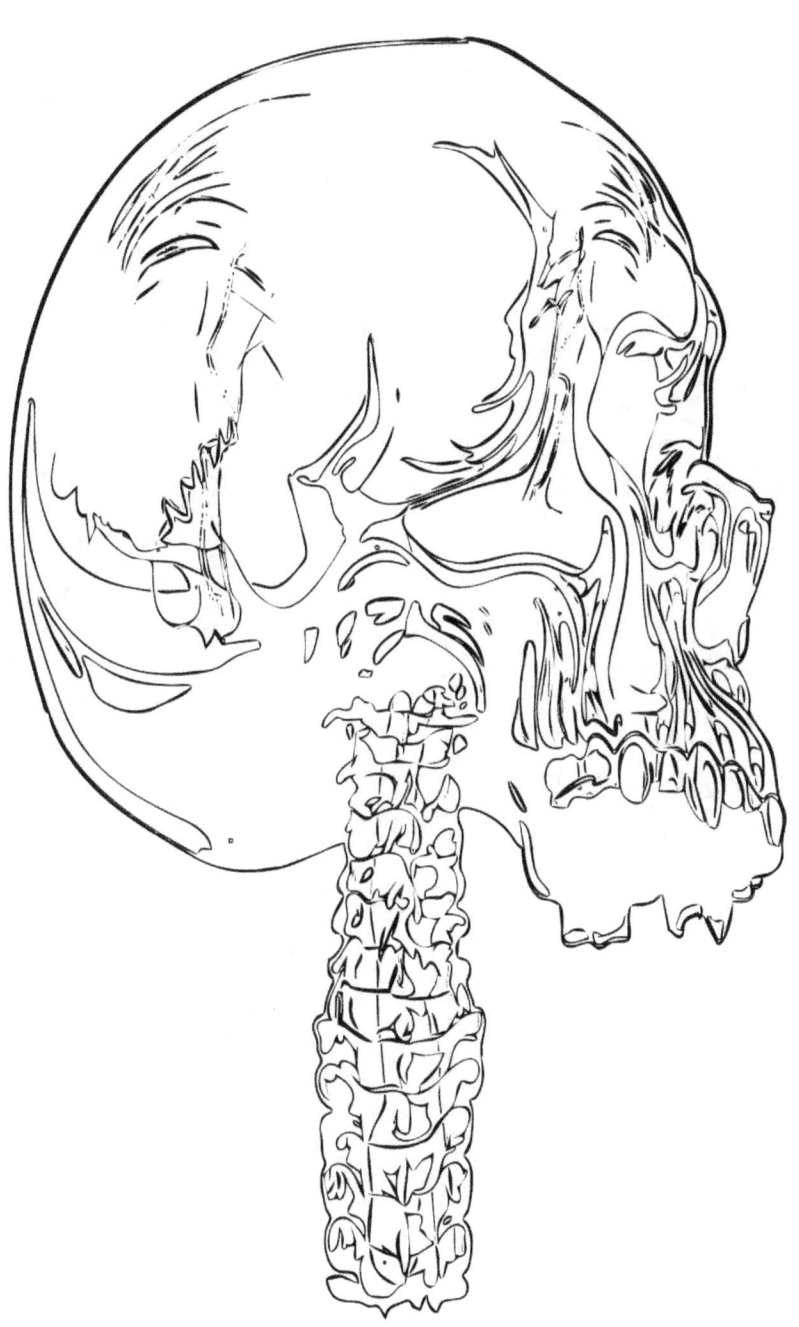

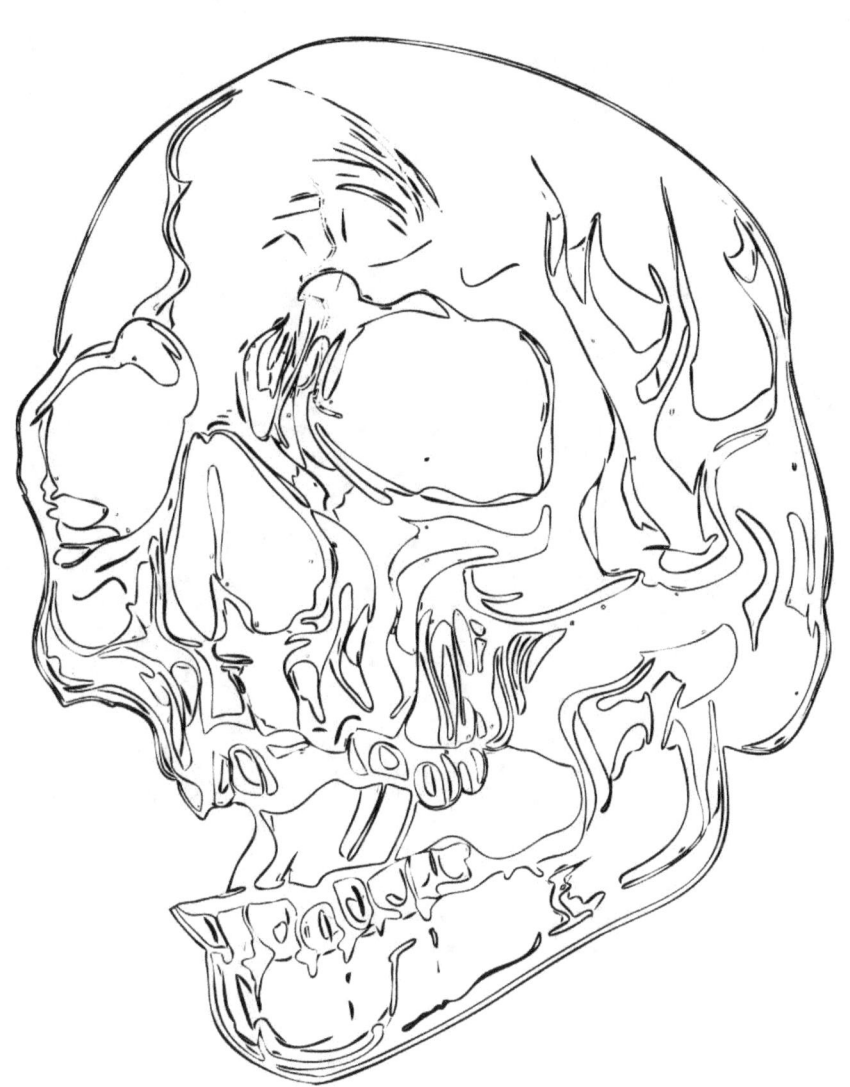

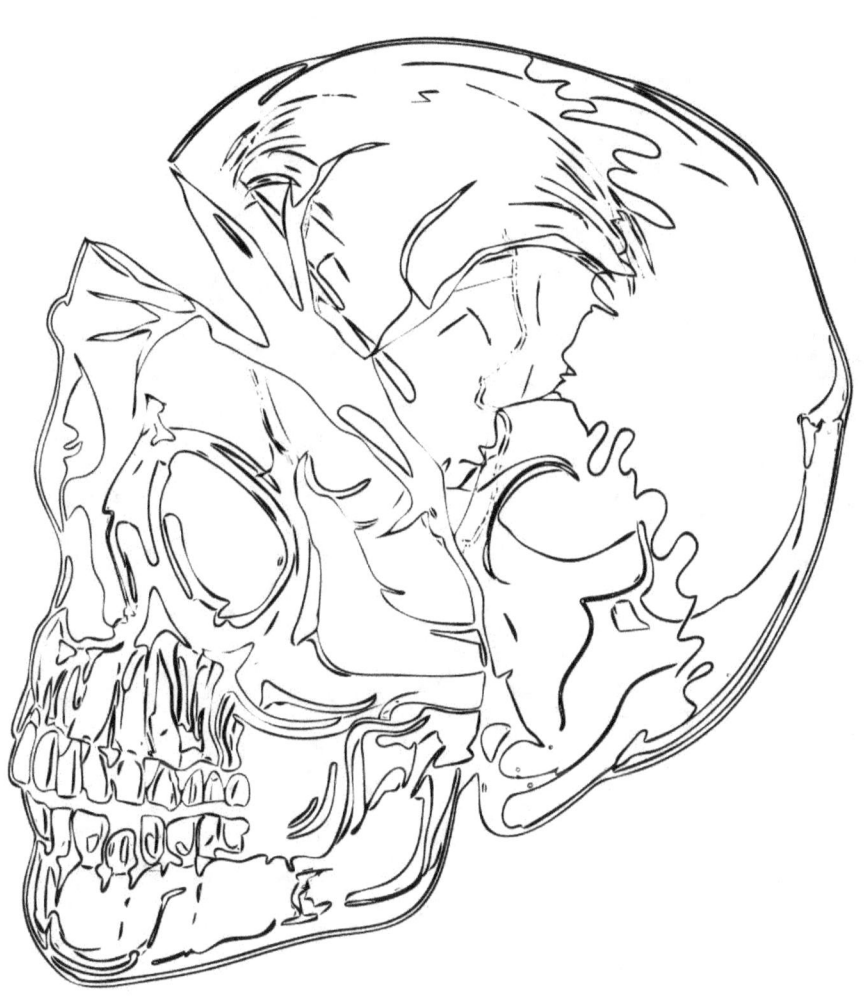

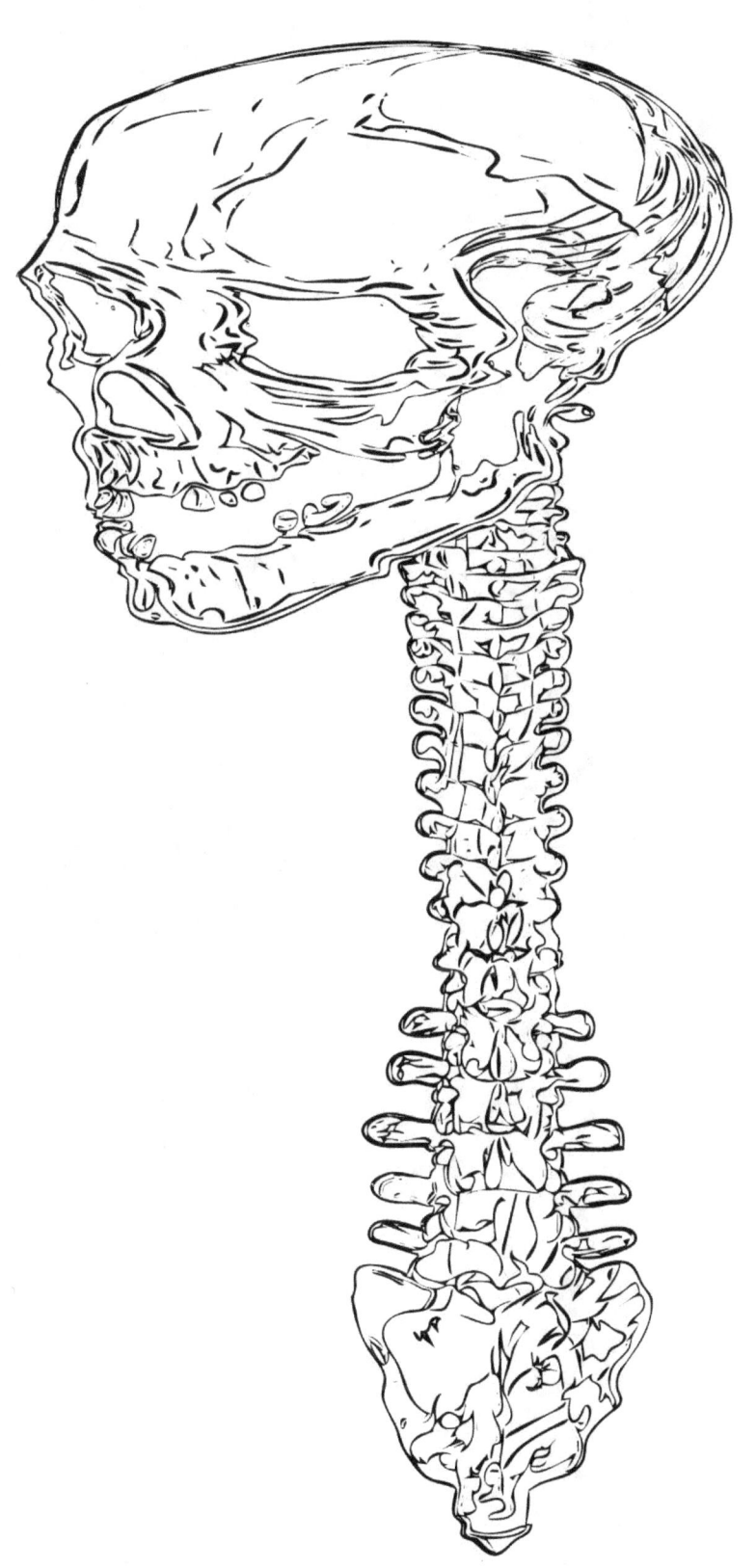

www.ingramcontent.com/pod-product-compliance
Lightning Source LLC
Chambersburg PA
CBHW081413170526
45166CB00010B/3318

* 9 7 8 1 5 1 9 5 0 9 5 6 7 *